M000035113

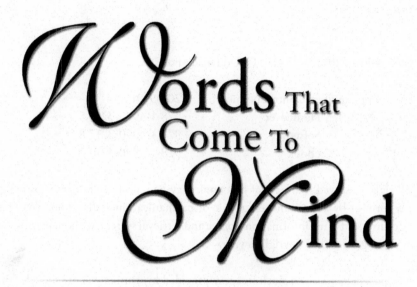

Words That Come To Mind

THE COLLECTION

LENORE C. UDDYBACK-FORTSON

Copyright © 2014 by Lenore C. Uddyback-Fortson.

Library of Congress Control Number:		2014910112
ISBN:	Hardcover	978-1-4990-3218-5
	Softcover	978-1-4990-3217-8
	eBook	978-1-4990-3219-2

All rights reserved. No part of this book may be reproduced or transmitted in any form or by any means, electronic or mechanical, including photocopying, recording, or by any information storage and retrieval system, without permission in writing from the copyright owner.

Any people depicted in stock imagery provided by Thinkstock are models, and such images are being used for illustrative purposes only.
Certain stock imagery © Thinkstock.

This book was printed in the United States of America.

Cover photographed by Jonathan Duncklee.

Rev. date: 08/22/2014

To order additional copies of this book, contact:
Xlibris LLC
1-888-795-4274
www.Xlibris.com
Orders@Xlibris.com
538111

Contents

WORDS THAT HEAL

WORDS THAT INSPIRE

WORDS THAT RENEW

WORDS OF THE NEXT GENERATION

Dedication

This book is dedicated to:

Jesus, who died so that I might have life more abundantly.
My mom, who fed my creativity and nourished my love of poetry.
Wes and Noah, who give me purpose and bring me joy.
The chorus of voices that echoed encouragement
for me to start this project.

Thoughts

What you have before you is a capsule of my thoughts, memories, dreams and revelations, spanning a 20-year period of my life—my love, my heartache and joy spilled onto every page. Some words came quickly as I sought refuge from unspeakable pain, tried to recapture the innocence of my childhood, daydreamed as I rode the train or walked to the rhythm of Philadelphia, Quebec, Boston, Baltimore and New York; sat on a beach, looked into the eyes of my life partner or a friend, or witnessed a beautiful love story. Others crystallized over time, shaped by each life lesson I learned; and finally, others were inspired by my journey on which I embarked when I began to truly understand who I am in Christ.

This book would not be possible were it not for the unending grace and mercy of my Lord and Savior, from whom all blessings flow, and the circle of family and friends with whom He has blessed me. I am indebted to all for the loving support shown to me and my work. I share each glimpse of my creativity with you openly, and pray that you will be touched in one way or another. Enjoy!

Words That Come To Mind

Images,
images that roll,
images that roll into

thoughts,
thoughts that bend,
thoughts that bend into

concepts,
concepts that take form;
form soon defined,
then refined by

words,
words that come,
words that come to mind.

Writer's Block

Words elude me.
They're hiding,
unwilling to conform to my imagination.
Escaping my mind,
they tease me,
leaving traces of thoughts I thought I had,
but can't quite remember.

Words That Define

I Can

I can do all things through Christ who strengthens me,
my head held high,
my eyes focused upward,
walking tall,
moving forward,
led by faith,
with the grace of the Holy Spirit holding me steady.

I can do all things through Christ who strengthens me,
without hesitation,
in spite of any obstacle,
in the face of persecution,
My God is always faithful.

I can do all things through Christ who strengthens me,
soaring above my aspirations,
leaving behind my inhibitions,
leaping over my limitations,
tightly gripping my Savior's hand.

I can do all things through Christ who strengthens me,
living,
loving,
laughing,
shouting praises to his name.

Yes, oh yes,
I can do all things through Christ who strengthens me,
and for that,
my life will never be
the same.

Tall, Black & Beautiful

I am tall, black and beautiful,
Fearfully and Wonderfully made.
My long lean body
reaches high into the sky,
while my coca-brown hue
dances merrily
through the sun's daily rays.

My mind,
already wide open,
broad and deep,
stretches further
with the slightest stimulation.

I don't cower
when I pass someone
with a cute, petite frame.
I just shoot arrow straight,
lift my head high,
and keep on steppin'.

Nor do I shrink in stature
to appease those
who don't feel comfortable with themselves;

Although I used to,
now I refuse to.

I don't hide
to play the game of the one
who can't match my intellect,

And I sure don't pretend to be something I'm not,
or wish to be something I'll never be.

I am,
Tall, black and beautiful;
Tall, black and beautiful;
Tall,
Black,
and beautiful,
now...deal with that!

On This Day

On this day
at this time,
I extend to you
my hand,
my heart,
my life,
reaching to grip yours,
a grip tightened
by faith and submission.

On this day,
all my fears have been drenched
with peace and everlasting hope,
moved deeply by your love,
tickled by funny memories,
secret smiles and gentle giggles.

On this day,
our new path
uncoils
from our long-winding history;
a journey
only for God to navigate,
as we follow blindly and boldly.

On this day,
at this very moment,
I stand
ready,
committed and
devoted to you
and you only.

Autumn

When Autumn comes,
life stops to take a breath,
the leaves rejoice
with an explosion of colors;
warm, inviting colors,
from candlelight and sunsets.

When Autumn comes,
all that was then is no longer;
a new day of reflection has arrived.

Hot, lazy days,
warm, frenzied nights,
replaced with a spell
serene and soothing;
cool winds blow,
awakening the weary,
whispering promises of another day,
a new day,
when Autumn comes.

Early Risers

When morning yawns
we break,
stealing a moment
of the earth's silence,
moving swiftly through
our own suspension of time,
glancing at distant companions,
overtaken
by unfamiliar peace.

Locomotive Daydreams

Endless images sneak into
my stained, two-way picture,
and I catch
an intoxicating montage
of lazy afternoon backdrops
drawing me into
a new-era fantasy
free of the day-to-day grip,
takes me on a mind trip,
island breeze,
dancing trees,
soft touches by a lover's lips.

Hypnotic rhythm of churning steel
indulges me,
lulls me,
transcends me to another existence,
no need for any resistance,
until the shriek of the brakes
snaps my gaze,
signaling that I've reached my stop.

Peace

My place of peace
summons the solitude
I covet every morning,
inviting quiet moments of clarity.

I go and gaze deep
into the reflection
of its surroundings;
losing minutes,
hypnotized by faithful ripples
that trouble a lazy surface.

Time snaps the trappings
of the day,
clearing the hazy debris of thoughts
that bombard my spirit,
and I am
free,
open to dream,
to anticipate
and to usher
my long-awaited share of contentment.

Words That Endear

Wings of Gold

You cradled me
when I was new to this world,
and lay helpless,
starved for protection
from all that was unfamiliar.

As I grew,
and the novelty of familiarity
grew tired,
your arms transformed into wings—Wings of gold;

So strong
that when I faltered or fell,
they lifted me
and again placed me firmly on my feet.

So gentle,
that the slightest touch,
would soothe my spirit
and calm my inner uproar.

So broad
that often
I stood in awe,
amazed at the many lives you saved.

So resilient
that in spite of the most crushing blow,
they soon regained
their beauty and grace.

And though your wings have taken you
to another place now—your resting place,
I know they'll always be with me,

For each day,
as the sunlight
splashes through my window,
announcing morning's arrival,
I'll search for the reflection
of your wings of gold
and bask in your warm embrace.

Legacy of Love

The years haven't erased
my longing for
your flesh-and-blood presence in my life;
A desire to see you, hear you, hug you,
just one more time—even for a second;
a forever-lingering wish
clinging to my heart, reminding me each
day—if only it were possible.

There are so many times
I need the safety of your smile,
or the comfort of your laugh
and wish I could bathe in the wisdom of your voice,
because now, for my precious gift from GOD,
I see through a mother's eyes,
feel with a mother's heart,
dream a mother's dream.

And there are times
I mad-dash to remember,
find traces
the spoken or the unspoken
that would guide me,
even for a second,
something you once said…once did,
that touched me, and now may equip me
to continue your legacy of love.

Face of Heaven

The face of Heaven
found me
in a matter of seconds,
smiling peace,
precious and pure,
securing all access to my heart.

And in that instant,
I was renewed,
transformed with purpose;

unmistakable,
unexplainable,
undeniable
joy
that leaves me floating,
dreaming of the possibilities.

My Sweet Prince

Your laughter ripples,
warming me inside from head to toe,
gently tugging
three hundred sixty degrees of my heart
as it locks my silly grin
permanently in place.

And when I see that smile,
brightness takes shape,
lighting a path of understanding
that redirects me
to what's really important.

My reflection shines
in your bubble of excitement,
uncontrollable giggles,
inquiring eyes,
insight,
dramatic pronouncements,
and unfailing love,
re-acquainting me with the little girl hiding inside.

My dreams for you run endless,
fly boundless,
traveling to places I've never been,
discovering things
that always seemed to elude me,
uncovering
what wasn't mine to find,
reaching heights
far above my reach,
capturing all life offers,
day by day,
moment by moment,
clothed in wisdom
through it all.

Sisters

We are sisters
bound by the blood
from which we were given life.

Paper dolls we dangle,
bearing the initials
K-L-K-L
separate but yet supportive,
independent yet interconnected,
different but yet really the same.

Eyes closed, holding our breath
we await the future's next move
when the wind blows,
only God knows,
We are sisters.

Remembering Quebec

We walked through streets…
streets pounded into history's tablet
page after page…retelling stories,
of discovery, war
defeat, victory.

Streets dusted with charm,
quaint and cozy,
simple and elegant.

We walked,
and inhaled the essence
of each new day,
musicians, jugglers and mimes,
appetizing teases
courting us around every corner.

We walked,
collecting delicious memories
of a new adventure.

Chelsea

I remember
you then,
bright-eyed,
seeking
full of life and wonderment,
sharing youthful wisdom,
delving into thoughts
found deep beneath those of
others your age.

I see you now,
a beautiful young woman,
those same bright eyes,
mirrors of early life lessons learned
reflecting the image
of the incredible woman
GOD created you to be.

I imagine
and celebrate your future,
full of promise,
rich with purpose,
directed by prayer,
propelled by GOD's grace.

Yesterday

Yesterday I journeyed
to a time
reminiscent of my childhood.
Memories dodged in and out of my mind,
daring me to recall the days
when youth and innocence tagged along,
teasing the future that didn't really matter at the time.

Everything was the same,
and yet so much was different.
I listened with my heart,
and distinctively heard
the melody of my mother's voice
and saw her face in the clouds that hovered
over my first homestead;
a place where life gave me
silly little girl smiles
and simple day-to-day adventures.

A gift I'll keep forever
as the past embraced the present
in harmony.

Inspired

Inspired you ask,
Am I not inspired by you?
So often, memories of you and me
running
laughing
joking
playing
caught up in the sights and sounds,
magnetic jazz melodies
and characters on stage
run courses through my mind,
all the while amazing me
that we could have become
best friends so fast,
but I have yet
to capture them on paper.

The future took me captive,
and far-removed me from those times,
but they seem just like yesterday,
and remind me of when
we were invincible,
capable of doing any and everything,
oblivious to the passage of time
and responsibilities awaiting us
just around the corner.

So in answer to your question,
Do you inspire me?
Of course you do,
You just did!

You are

You are a friend
without compromise,
without limitations,
without expectations,
without question.

You are a mom and a grand mom,
a cool one
to those whom you were given by nature,
and to the many you adopted in spirit,
seamlessly stitching your heart to another.

You are a joy;
your smile radiates light
that glows from within,
and warms whatever room you enter.

You are a wonder,
an example of what can happen
when someone isn't blinded
by what can't be done
or overcome in life.

You are
and always will be
a blessing
to me and to
everyone else fortunate enough
to cross your path.

Love will

Love will lead us
on adventures unseen
beyond our boundaries of comfort,
hands folded, clasped with commitment.

Love will lead us up and over
life's viscous terrains
prevailing with purpose…peace.

Together,
in step,
in sync,
to unmask
life's mysteries
marked solely for our destiny,
discovering each one
boldly,
firmly planted in faith.

It will take us to the pinnacle of nature's grandeur
to inhale the essence of all God's created,
despite a stance that defies our desire
to pursue it.

Sustaining us through wild waters,
calming storms,
leaving refreshing puddles
for us to dance through later.

Love will lead us back to one another
without trepidation
if ever we drift, daunted by circumstances,

Ours will be
a union unyielding,
buoyed by bountiful blessings,
if
and only if,
we let love lead us.

Celebrate The Milestone

Today we unwrap the gift of life
and its many intricacies.

Reflections
of triumphs and trials,
mistakes and memories,
laughter, labor and learned lessons,
smiles and seaside sunsets,
grainy sand, great plowing waves
Irish green, perennial gardens,
cool soil,
hands submerged in nature's therapy,
holiday cheer,
and ultimately, the love of family,
nourished, savored, perfected through generations.

Today we unwrap the gift of life
and celebrate the milestone
without regret, fear or frown,
but with a peace-filling bright light of hope
brought by the future—the exhale of understanding,
wisdom steadying our stance,
sending us assuredly
on the next stretch of our journey.

The Perfect Moment

Sweet joy splashed me,
reviving my creative instinct
with magnificent color-stroked images
and vibrant artistic brilliance—almost too awesome to behold,
prompting smile bursts
and heart-touched tears
beckoning songs of happiness
and unburied belly laughter,
at the perfect moment,
on the perfect day of girlfriend sharing,
preserving
what will become
a long-cherished lifetime memory.

Love Sonata

The day I glanced your way,
I shuddered at the pulse of your energy
and the intensity of your spirit,
became intrigued by your unquenchable passion
for discovering, savoring life's treasures.

When our eyes met,
I explored the depth
of your character...so strong,
solid,
sound,
pure,
resolved to be upright.

It was that day
that found me captured
by the romance
of all you have to offer
in the perfect stillness
of a quiet moment.

And in that moment,
my heart reached out
to feel the embrace of yours.
It was home,
and I caught a glimpse
of my partner,
my soul mate,
my best friend for life.

Love Notes

Melodious reminders
of how
when
and why
I gave you my heart,
and the tender way you accepted it
unconditionally
in exchange for yours.

A tune that I hum to myself
every time your name comes to mind,
I escape to our special
star-dusted night,
when the breeze was still
and the moon hovered near.

A sweet song stirred
by the touch of your hand,
and the way it fits so snugly in mine,
as if they were made
one to be part of the other.

The prayer that I have for our life together,
flowing limitless to a destination
only God knows.

Syncopated rhythms
that take us back
to our first glance,
our first smile,
our first kiss.

So when life seems too hectic,
too much to bear,
too much to sift,

we'll go running,
find a love note,
close our eyes,
relax
and drift.

Words That Heal

I Shed A Tear

I shed a tear for you today
when I opened my eyes
and realized
that you weren't there
to tell me you loved me;

a tear not unlike those
that fell last night
when I cried myself to sleep;

a tear laced with
the pain and sadness
that arrived when you left us,
and continue to be
my constant companions;

a tear that mirrors the hopes and dreams
we had for each other,
and is filled with
all of the good-byes
I hated to say
but had to;

a tear that stung my heart
as it rolled down my cheek,
hesitating first
before finally diving to its finish.

I shed a tear for you today,
and I'm sure that soon
another will follow.

Alone and Grown

I needed you
when I woke up today,
to hug my tears and sadness away,
to tell me again
that I'll be okay
alone and grown in this world.

I needed the sense of security
that you always seemed to provide for me.
You're the strong woman
I long to be
when I'm alone and grown in this world.

I'll never forget your flawless grace,
or how you lived by the rule,
"There's a time and place,"
or the deep sense of love
that filled your embrace,
or the joy that your laugher would bring.

I long for the day
when we'll meet again,
as mother to daughter,
as friend to friend.
But I know I've got things
yet to do until then,
alone and grown in this world.

So I'll whisper a prayer of thanks to God
and send it on the wind's trail;
and watch as it flutters,
as it dips, and dives, as it soars and as it sails.

And I know you'll be watching and waiting,
for the me-I'm-to-be to unveil.
And I'll not give up hope
or forget what you've taught:
"Lean on Jesus,
and although you're grown,
you won't be alone in this world."

Missing Mommy Moment

A missing Mommy moment
sideswiped me today
when I wasn't paying attention.

Snuck up on me,
and
before I knew it,
I was rattled,
tossed around,
shook upside down,
turned inside out,
bounced from wall to wall
to wall to wall to wall,
all in a matter of seconds.

Til finally,
with a hint of compassion,
it released me,
left me breathless,
my emotional reservoir drained,
and I thought it had hit drought level ages ago.

Yeah, it left me and
joined self-pity,
and good ole depression
who had long-tortured joy into submission.
Together they taunted me,
and taunted me,
and taunted me,
til finally,
whipped by fatigue and drowned in my tears,
I slept.

On the Verge

I'm lonely,
tho I know I'm not alone.

Sad,
tho my heart is filled with joy.

Pensive,
tho I still rejoice.

Halted,
tho I am moving forward.

I miss you,
tho I know you're still with me.

I'm living for the moment,
tho longing for the future.

I'm concentrating on the here and now,
tho clinging to a precious memory.

I'm all cried out,
tho always on the verge.

To Gary... Rest Well My Angel

You were mine
and I knew you,
as no one else would,
as no one else could;

And I loved you,
for so long it seemed,
longer than time would suggest;

And I held you,
close and safe,
warm and protected,
perfect and still;

And you touched me,
deeper than I thought possible,
in places I only then discovered.

Our bond,
so real,
so strong,
hand to hand,
heart to heart,
energy exchanged,
connecting in our special way,

Each day
collecting memories
forever captured in my heart,
my mind
my soul.
Rest well my angel.

A Scene Spied Through Lonely Eyes

In the midst of a crowded city street,
I sit on an old wooden bench,
its place highlighted
by a crack in worn cement.

Planks,
smaller than they used to be
reminisce about the couples
who once carved their claim.

I sit tracing the letters slowly,
wondering,
wishing,
held down by,
trapped within,
my heart's cemented sadness.

People stream in waves,
engrossed in conversation,
with pasted generic smiles,
immersed in thought.

I watch the scene alone from a distance
as though it were projected from a 70mm.
Tears of self-pity distort the images.
Comfort music
drowns out all sound around me
and wrestles my amplified thoughts til they cower.
The picture fades to black.
Cut!

Ode to Deptford High

Teenage miseries blister,
pain rubbed raw,
time spent
awkward,
anxious,
nervous,
nestled,
suffocating suburbia
locked down by
time-warped, ill-fated souls
clamoring about when or if
they were eva gonna overcome.
Oh hmmm, My bad…that was me wondering.

Mean nobodies
pretending to be somebody
doing nothing…heading nowhere.

Honorary Klansmen and women
disguised as educators,
stuck in,
yet wanting to be anywhere but
small, small, small town USA.

My own,
never reaching for the stars,
fixated instead
on the invisible noose they tooled to try and hold me back,

But I broke free,
broke free and ran... so fast,
right into the arms of another racist neighborhood,
New England.

But that was years ago.
Time brought
layers upon layers
of focused healing,
until something said, seen or heard
recently rubbed me the wrong way,
and it didn't take long for me to realize
that old wounds burrow just beneath the surface.

Treasured

Our friendship was treasured
although I didn't always say it
because despair often held my tongue
and impaired my vision,
blurring the blessings right in front of me,
weakening our foundation of sisterhood,
making it fragile and brittle.

But don't ever doubt
whether you took and held your rightful place in my heart,
because I can say without question—you did,
energizing my dim spirits on more than one occasion,
challenging my doubts and the limits I placed on myself,
questioning my distorted outlook in such a valued way.

The promise of our renewed friendship remains constant.
It cradles my hope,
shields my sadness,
and fuels my prayers
that reveal a deep longing for another opportunity
to tell you, show you,
erase all evidence to the contrary,
say with and without words,
just how much it is
I truly love you.

Words That Inspire

The Gift of a Spirit

A quiet, gentle spirit
came to us in love.

Humble,
Honest,
sharing words,
simple,
powerful,
seasoned with wisdom,
The wisdom of God
spirit evoking,
propelling saints
to share the good news of salvation
to all within reach;

And many were touched,
and many found Christ,
and many were changed.

And so,
as he came,
he now leaves
following an obedient heart
with purpose to serve,
awaiting
all that God has in store
for this gentle spirit,
so graciously given
to us
but for a moment.

Mighty Shepherd

A shepherd after God's own heart,
a mighty shepherd,
stands willing to meet his destiny
'living' worship,
leading a peculiar people,
a royal priesthood.

Trained in the world,
his brilliance sparkled,
clearing a path
through thick, uncharted territory;
at times, the first, the only...
the doctor,
embodying Jehovah Raphah, God has healed;

And bodies were healed, and fears quieted
because of his mind,
his skill,
his grace.

Perfected in the spirit,
his life shines brighter,
a living example,
illuminating wisdom that streams through poetic verse,
pours from his lips,
offering a specific word from God;
and souls are mended,
because of his heart,
his humility,
his grace...loving pastor, thoughtful teacher, gracious leader.

A shepherd after God's own heart
stands ready to march his flock into battle
with his full armor,
forever faithful,
proclaiming sweet praises,
exalting Christ, his Savior.

A Dream

A dream,
echoed in the wind of possibility,
giving way
to a life-stirring breeze
awakening many
shackled by fear,
thirsting for freedom,
long-scorched, whipped, hanged to die,
brutalized by oppression.

A dream
realized by chance,
herald by a silent scream,
pleading, pleading, pleading for truth
in the ugly face of lies,
injustice.

A dream
fortified by quiet strength,
power,
made clear through
each and every utterance.

A dream
tattooed with blood,
the slain indelibly etched at the core,
our country's bruised soul.

A dream...to be revered,
protected every day,
every minute, every hour, every second,
our blessed existence to be passed
generation to generation to generation,
a priceless heirloom.

A dream
begun in the heart of one man—God cleared for him
the path he followed.
He was...a true leader.
He is...a legacy
burning eternal.

'Dream Speaker'

A dream speaker
arose before the world,
daring to disturb the status quo,
knowing,
showing
just because it was,
didn't mean it was supposed to be;
didn't mean it had to be.

He unleashed a vision
that tore through a binding net of hatred.
Each of his carefully-crafted words
hung high with promise,
filling the air,
waving triumphantly,
a banner of truth, peace,
blanketing a cold and battered people,
nourishing a nation hungry for hope.

He was a dream speaker
who sought dream catchers,
warriors charged to carry on,
to live his vision,
to fulfill his dream,

Dream catchers,
like you?
like me?

Are we living his dream,
or
just lost in an illusion?

Do we hold his banner,
or
just bear false bravado?

Are we the people he envisioned,
or
simply a silhouette of the possibility that lies within each of us?

A Message to the African-American Family

Hold fast to the memory
of those who sacrificed,
cried, ran, bled and died
for us,
calloused by freedom,
defying captors ignited with ignorance, envy

Hold tight to one another,
unified,
deliberate,
focused,
armed with pride.

Hold strong to the ideals
prescribed by our elders,
rooted in faith,
unyielding to temptation.

Hold on 'cause
tho troubled times abound,
God's promises always resound
with brilliant light
and triumphant hope
in the hearts of those who believe.

Tomorrow's Woman

Here
I stand,
tomorrow's woman
of
purpose, potential and principle.

Reaching for heights unknown,
no longer tethered to limits
that once held me just below
an invisible glass ceiling.

Guided by God,
I embrace opportunity
fearlessly
with the weight of every ounce of my energy.

Right now I spend my days
collecting girlish memories—friendships and laughter,
outside games,
Saturday malls,
dancing and singing to the music of my childhood,
all while trying to shut out
angry images
of violence and loss
that demand attention
on our societal stage;

Ringing gunshots replacing school bells,
innocence lost,
desperate to drown the constant clamor
that signals hatred's persistence.

I long for tomorrow,
my time to make a difference with the gifts I possess.
Dripping with dreams,
I take giant strides toward the future
determined to defy stereotypical devices
designed to distract me.

Take notice!
Make way for me!
Anticipate the force of my impact!
Remember,
I am
Tomorrow's woman.

Change of the Hour

With a change of the hour
adventure is unleashed without limitations,
sky bound,
sea deep,
rich lounging pastures,
anticipating your arrival.

One more glance?
No... that time has passed!
Forward my friend
is the only direction.
Go boldly without fear;
proudly, knowing your work is done;
swiftly, time never hesitates;
peacefully, resting on the joy new days will bring.
Go, but never forget, never, ever forget.

Morning

In the silence of morning,
I catch my mind racing
to imagined adventures
in my future.

Leaping over hurdles that spring up
like wildfire,
clinging to the unchanging hand of my Savior.

In the wake of the sun's first appearance,
I dance through mind-eye images,
mazes of foggy memories that often appear,
reminding me of where I've been,
encouraging me to keep on moving toward the dreams,
whose promises keep me company.

Words That Renew

Next Chapter

I awakened this morning
to a new chapter of life, of love,
When the radiance of your perfect light
stroked my brow,
electrifying everything within me.

And I was lifted from the sustained slumber of sadness
I long allowed to steal my joy.

I now accept with praise
the gifts you've given,
and present them as my simple offering to you.

Stepping into the sunlight of my destiny—my Hallelujah Horizon,
I plant my feet firmly
in the peace of your promises,
my spirit shielded by your love and grace.

I yield my will to yours this day,
moment by moment by moment,
no longer succumbing
to the strength of my yesterdays,
or cowering,
hiding from the powerful unknown
of my tomorrows.

Instead,
I stand rejoicing,
ready to follow
the path of righteousness
you've stretched out before me.

O Lord

I long to hear your voice
O Lord,
and anticipate the sound of life
speaking peace beyond measure
directly to the core of my heart,
breathing new hope into
my strained and long-suffering spirit.

I long to see your face
O Lord,
to hide myself without shame
in the embrace
of your glory and grace,
humbly basking in
a single moment of worship.

I long to feel your presence
O lord,
so that I,
if but only for a second,
can know without question,
the wonder of pure joy.

It is you I seek to mirror
O Lord,
your heart
I want to know and share,
your purpose for me
I desire to fulfill,
your will
I pray
be done,
Amen.

Swept Away

When I think about how you saved me,
kept me,
nestled me
in the palm of your hand,
strengthening me,
surrounding me with your protection,
guiding me, leading me through the power of your spirit,
shielding me with the breadth of your wisdom.

When I ponder the very ways
your hand has remained upon me,
covered me,
shrouded me with your love,
even when I tried to turn, walk away,
knowing better, feigning indifference,
stuck in my selfish, unyielding stance.

When I stop, and really look back
with open, honest eyes
that see without filter;
fully take in
how you gifted me,
lovingly prepared me—even through hardship and trial,
for the journey you planned my life to take,
I am swept away
by the overwhelming current of joy your blessings bring,
and without warning,
thankful tears stream in submission.

New Eyes of Hope

Brightness blinds me,
warms me,
leads me,
holds me,
encourages me
with each step I take toward triumph.

Dark, dismal days
release ambitions,
once arrested by fear,
and purpose declares victory.
I am moved to tears.

A deafening mantra of promise materializes,
removing all doubt, and life takes shape
in ways only realized in dreams—vivid,
active,
unashamed,
perfectly orchestrated images
that appear in living color right before my eyes,
eyes once downcast,
now lifted in the direction
from whence cometh my help;
and it comes,
and I can now see it,
through my new eyes of hope.

Sweet Remembrances

The sun smiled on me this morning,
warming my face and tickling my ear
as it whispered sweet remembrances
of God's Glory,
God's Grace,
the many ways God has touched me
and made me whole,
extending His holy hand
over the damaged areas of my soul,
those in need of repair.

And there were many,
still are many
in need of His hand;
areas I remain too afraid to explore,
or even face,
despite His assurance.

So patiently He waits
for my faith to lead me
to the place
where my Heavenly Father
always demonstrates
His unconditional love,
compassion,
deep understanding of my thoughts, fears and cares.

There, He waits
for me to cast them onto Him,
to take His yoke with ease,
and with rest,
because He cares for me.

The Deep Well of Wisdom

With outstretched hands,
a wide-open heart,
and a quiet, willing spirit,
I kneel,
anticipating the presence
of my Heavenly Father.

Humbly on my knees
I again come
to taste and to see
that the Lord is good.

I remain,
longing for even a drop of the dew
that clings to His deep well of wisdom,
a word
released in a whisper,
a still, small voice,
echoing volumes,
offering a jarring splash of life's true meaning,
re-affirming my purpose,
refreshing my dusty core,
leaving me wanting,
yearning,
crying out for His full embrace of Glory.

And yet,
in a moment,
time suspends,
and I am filled.

I arise,
my mind renewed,
and once more,
I am ready to face the world.

Triumphant Return

No trumpets,
drums,
or fanfare
announced the occasion,
but my heart rejoiced
and sang praises to the heavens.

Words Of The Next Generation

Walking Through Life with Confidence

By Noah C. Fortson

Confidence is something you gain.
It can be constructed through life randomly.
When walking through a world that is not very confident,
People tried to sing your lullaby by saying you will die.
You ignored and said, "Okay, I am not afraid."

Your confidence was unique.
It was like you are walking through life with confidence.
You knew God is walking with you forever and ever more.
You know that because every time life threw a fast ball,
You knew how to hit a home run.
You intentionally walk through death itself.
You are almost dead one minute, alive the next.

People have been mocking you about
your walking right near death.
When your parents died, it was devastation
But it was okay, you had confidence.
You were resourceful.
You knew how to handle death.
You tried surveying death, but you didn't want to go.
Previously, you had been healthy.
Now you sleep peacefully.
You walk through life with confidence.
That is who you are.

CPSIA information can be obtained
at www.ICGtesting.com
Printed in the USA
BVOW03s1704060617

486154BV00001B/27/P